Fossils

written by John Lockyer

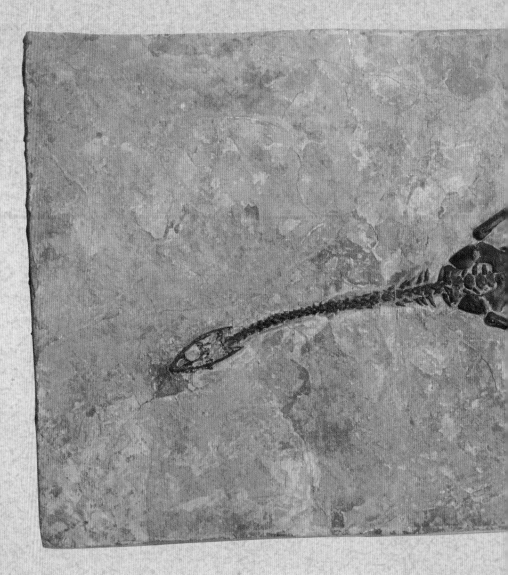

Fossils are important signs of ancient life. They are found preserved in rock in many parts of the world.

Fossils can be tiny plants and animals, or enormous dinosaur footprints and bones. Fossils are millions of years old.

A fossil can begin to form when an animal dies.
Over a long time, the dead animal's body is
covered with many layers of sand and mud.

Then the sand, the mud, and the animal's bones slowly turn into hard rock. Sometimes, millions of years later, the fossil is uncovered.

body fossil

Body fossils are the whole body or parts of the body of a plant or an animal. Imprint fossils are plants and trees that have rotted and left an imprint in rock. Trace fossils are markings, like footprints, tracks, burrows, and nests, made by ancient animals.

Fossils are found in strange places. Sea shell fossils have been discovered in the mountains. Scientists believe the mountains must have been under the sea long, long ago.

amber

Body fossils have been found in amber. Amber is the hardened sap that comes from ancient trees. Tiny animals became fossils by being trapped in the tree sap, and then buried for millions of years.

Many fossils are found in places with bare rock. Rocky shores, stream beds, caves, and sea cliffs have lots of fossils. These fossils are uncovered when water washes away part of the rocks.

Scientists work together to uncover a new fossil. Paleontologists decide what the fossil is. Geologists decide how old the rocks are. Technicians use small chisels, picks, and brushes to clean away rock, dirt, and dust from small fossils. Sometimes explosives and jack-hammers are used to uncover large fossils.

If the paleontologists find enough bones, they can put the skeleton of the animal together. Any missing bones are replaced with plastic copies.

Fossils show us what plants and animals have lived on Earth. Many of these plants and animals have become extinct. Dinosaurs are extinct, but we know a lot about them from their fossils.

Dinosaur footprints show how fast the dinosaur moved and if it stood on two legs or four. Paleontologists built a stegosaurus skeleton from a fossil found in the USA. They know that dinosaurs made nests, and their young hatched from eggs.

After many plants and animals were buried together millions of years ago, they slowly changed into fossil fuels. Coal and oil and natural gas have all been formed from fossils.

Fossil fuels are mined or pumped up from the ground and burned for energy. Fossils may be millions of years old, but we still use some of them every day.

oil drills

You can make your own fossil with clay.
You need: white clay, a hard shape like a shell,
paint, and a paintbrush.
1   Roll some clay into a ball.
2   Press your shape or shell into the clay.
3   Remove the shape or shell.
4   Leave the clay until it is hard.
5   Paint your fossil to make it look more real.